A LOVE WORTH WORTH GIVING TO YOU at Christmas

MAX LUCADO

W PUBLISHING GROUP™

www.wpublishinggroup.com

A Division of Thomas Nelson, Inc.
www.ThomasNelson.com

A LOVE WORTH GIVING TO YOU AT CHRISTMAS

Unless otherwise indicated, Scripture quotations used in this book are from the Holy Bible, New Century Version (NCV), copyright © 1987, 1988, 1991 by Word Publishing, Dallas, Texas 75234. Used by permission.

Other Scripture references are from the following sources:

The Holy Bible, New International Version (NIV). Copyright © 1973, 1978, 1984, International Bible Society. Used by permission of Zondervan Bible Publishers. The Living Bible (TLB), copyright © 1971 by Tyndale House Publishers, Wheaton, Ill. Used by permission. The Message (MSG), copyright © 1993. Used by permission of NavPress Publishing Group. The New King James Version (NKJV). Copyright © 1982 by Thomas Nelson, Inc. Used by permission. All rights reserved. New American Standard Bible (NASB), © 1960, 1977 by the Lockman Foundation. The Good News Bible: The Bible in Today's English Version (TEV) © 1976 by the American Bible Society.

The content of this book is adapted from previously published works. Consult the permission page in the back of the book for a complete list.

Produced with the assistance of The Livingstone Corporation. Project staff includes David R. Veerman and Betsy Todt Schmitt.

ISBN 0-8499-4404-X

Library of Congress Cataloging-in-Publication Data

Lucado, Max.
  A love worth giving to you at Christmas / Max Lucado.
    p. cm.
  ISBN 0-8499-4404-X (pbk.)
  1. God—Love. 2. Love—Religious aspects—Christianity. 3. Christian life. I. Title.
  BT140 .L84 2002
  231'.6—dc21   2002012960

Printed in the United States of America
02 03 04 05 OPM 9 8 7 6 5 4 3 2 1

CONTENTS

✳

THE SEASON OF GIVING

Every good and perfect gift is from above, coming down from the Father of the heavenly lights, who does not change like shifting shadows. (James 1:17 NIV).

Extravagant Giving

We delight in giving our loved ones extravagant gifts, don't we? Especially at Christmas. Yes, we give gifts throughout the year—birthdays, anniversaries, and other special occasions—but at Christmastime, we put a little more effort into finding that extra special gift for that special person, or persons, in our lives. An engagement ring. A family portrait. A special edition leather-bound book. A set of golf clubs. Diamond earrings. A puppy. Whatever the gift might be, we want it to be a bountiful expression of our love.

Maybe it has something to do with the lavishness of the gift that first Christmas morning, the extravagance of love that came in the form of a tiny, helpless newborn. Consider the gift for a moment, what Jesus *really* did. He swapped a spotless castle for a grimy stable. He exchanged the worship of angels for the company of killers. He could hold the universe in his palm but gave it up to float in the womb of a maiden.

If you were God, would you sleep on straw, nurse from a breast, and be clothed in a diaper? Christ did.

If you knew that only a few would care that you came, would you still come? If you knew that those you loved would laugh in your face, would you still care? If you knew that the tongues you made would mock you, the mouths you made would spit at you, the hands you made would crucify you, would you still make them? Christ did. Would you regard the immobile and invalid more important than yourself? Jesus did.

He humbled himself. He went from commanding angels to sleeping in the straw. From holding stars to clutching Mary's finger. The palm that held the universe took the nail of a soldier.

Why? Because that's what love does. It puts the beloved before itself. Your soul was more important than his blood. Your eternal life was more important than his earthly life. Your place in heaven was more important to him than his place in heaven, so he gave up his so you could have yours.

And that's what extravagant giving is all about—love, God's love, a love that knows no bounds, no limits, no end. The Christmas kind of love. The type of love we are commanded to give to others: "So now I am giving you a new commandment: Love each other. Just as I have loved you, you should love each other" (John 13:34 NLT). A love worth giving to others. To you.

There's a problem, though. How can you give something that you never truly received?

He went from commanding angels to sleeping in the straw. From holding stars to clutching Mary's finger. The palm that held the universe took the nail of a soldier.

A Love
Worth Giving

WE LOVE EACH OTHER AS A RESULT
OF HIS LOVING US FIRST.
(1 JOHN 4:19 NLT)

The Party

The Bible provides insight into what I call the 7:47 principle, "A person who is forgiven little shows only little love" (Luke 7:47 NLT). The setting is a party in Capernaum. Jesus is the guest of honor, and well, you'll pick up the rest as we enter the room.

Could two people be more different?

He is looked up to. She is looked down on.

He is a church leader. She is a streetwalker.

He makes a living promoting standards. She's made a living breaking them.

He's hosting the party. She's crashing it.

Ask the other residents of Capernaum to point out the more pious of the two, and they'll pick Simon. Why, after all, he's a student of theology, a man of the cloth. Anyone would pick him. Anyone, that is, except Jesus. Jesus knew them both. And Jesus would pick the woman. Jesus does pick the woman. And, what's more, he tells Simon why.

Not that Simon wants to know. His mind is elsewhere. *How did this whore get in my house?* He doesn't know whom to yell at first, the woman or the servant who let her in. After all, this dinner is a formal affair. Invitation only. Upper crust. Crème de la crème. Who let the riffraff in?

Simon is angry. *Just look at her—groveling at*

Jesus' feet. Kissing them, no less! Why, if Jesus were who he says he is, he would have nothing to do with this woman.

One of the lessons Simon learned that day was this: Don't think thoughts you don't want Jesus to hear. For Jesus heard them, and when he did, he chose to share a few of his own.

"Simon," he said to the Pharisee, "I have something to say to you."

"All right, Teacher," Simon replied, "go ahead."

Then Jesus told him this story: "A man loaned money to two people—five hundred pieces of silver to one and fifty pieces to the other. But neither of them could repay him, so he kindly forgave them both, canceling their debts. Who do you suppose loved him more after that?"

Simon answered, "I suppose the one for whom he canceled the larger debt."

"That's right," Jesus said. Then he turned to the woman and said to Simon, "Look at this woman kneeling here. When I entered your home, you didn't offer me water to wash the dust from my feet, but she has washed them with her tears and wiped them with her hair. You didn't give me a kiss of greeting, but she has kissed my feet again and again from the time I first came in. You neglected the courtesy of olive oil to anoint my head, but she has anointed my feet with rare perfume. I tell you, her sins— and they are many—have been forgiven, so she has shown me much love. But a person who is forgiven little shows only little love" (Luke 7:40–47 NLT).

Simon invites Jesus to his house but treats him like an unwanted step-uncle. No customary courtesies. No kiss of greeting. No washing his feet. No oil for his head.

Or, in modern terms, no one opened the

I TELL YOU, HER

SINS—AND THEY ARE

MANY—HAVE BEEN

FORGIVEN, SO SHE

HAS SHOWN ME

MUCH LOVE.

door for him, took his coat, or shook his hand. Count Dracula has better manners.

Simon does nothing to make Jesus feel welcome. The woman, however, does everything that Simon didn't. We aren't told her name. Just her reputation—a sinner. A prostitute most likely. She has no invitation to the party and no standing in the community. (Imagine a hooker in a tight dress showing up at the parsonage during the pastor's Christmas party. Heads turn. Faces blush. Gasp!)

But people's opinions didn't stop her from coming. It's not for them she has come. It's for him. Her every move is measured and meaningful. Each gesture extravagant. She puts her cheek to his feet, still dusty from the path. She has no water, but she has tears. She has no towel, but she has her hair. She uses both to bathe the feet of Christ. As one translation reads, "she rained tears" on his feet (v. 44 MSG). She opens a vial of perfume, perhaps her only possession of worth, and massages it into his skin. The aroma is as inescapable as the irony.

The Problem

You'd think Simon of all people would show such love. Is he not the reverend of the church, the student of Scripture? But he is harsh, distant. You'd think the woman would avoid Jesus. Is she not the woman of the night, the town hussy? But she can't resist him. Simon's "love" is calibrated and stingy. Her love, on the other hand, is extravagant and risky.

How do we explain the difference between the two? Training? Education? Money? No, for Simon has outdistanced her in all three.

But there is one area in which the woman leaves him eating dust. Think about it. What one discovery has she made that Simon hasn't? What one treasure does she cherish that Simon doesn't? Simple. God's love. We don't know when she received it. We aren't told how she heard about it. Did she overhear Jesus' words "Your Father is merciful" (Luke 6:36 NIV)? Was she nearby when Jesus had compassion on the widow of Nain? Did someone tell her how Jesus touched lepers and turned tax collectors into disciples? We don't know. But we know this. She came thirsty. Thirsty from guilt. Thirsty from regret. Thirsty from countless nights of making love and finding none. She came thirsty.

And when Jesus hands her the goblet of grace, she drinks. She doesn't just taste or nip. She doesn't dip her finger and lick it or take the cup and sip it. She lifts the liquid to her lips and drinks, gulping and swallowing like the parched pilgrim she is. She drinks until the mercy flows down her chin and onto her neck and chest. She

SHE COMES THIRSTY.

AND WHEN JESUS

HANDS HER THE

GOBLET OF GRACE,

SHE DRINKS.

drinks until every inch of her soul is moist and soft. She comes thirsty and she drinks. She drinks deeply.

Simon, on the other hand, doesn't even know he is thirsty. People like Simon don't need grace; they analyze it. They don't request mercy; they debate and prorate it. It wasn't that Simon couldn't be forgiven; he just never asks to be.

The Principle

So while she drinks up, he puffs up. While she has ample love to give, he has no love to offer. Why? The 7:47 Principle. Read again verse 47 of chapter 7: "A person who is forgiven little shows only little love." Just like the jumbo jet, the 7:47 Principle has wide wings. Just like the aircraft, this truth can lift you to another level. Read it one more time. "A person who is forgiven little shows only little love." In other words, we can't give what we've never received. If we've never received love, how can we love others?

But, oh, how we try! As if we can conjure up love by the sheer force of will. As if there is within us a distillery of affection that lacks only a piece of wood or a hotter fire. We poke it and stoke it with resolve. What's our typical strategy for treating a troubled relationship? Try harder.

"My spouse needs my forgiveness? I don't know how, but I'm going to give it."

"I don't care how much it hurts, I'm going to be nice to that bum."

"I'm supposed to love my neighbor? Okay. By golly, I will."

So we try. Teeth clinched. Jaw firm. We're going to love if it kills us! And it may do just that.

Could it be we are missing a step? Could it be that the first step of love is not toward them but toward him? Could it be that the secret to loving is receiving? You give love by first receiving it. "We love, because He first loved us" (1 John 4:19 NASB).

Long to be more loving? Begin by accepting your place as a dearly loved child. "Be imitators of God, therefore, as dearly loved children and live a life of love, just as Christ loved us" (Eph. 5:1–2 NIV).

Want to learn to forgive? Then consider how you've been forgiven. "Be kind and compassionate to one another, forgiving each other, just as in Christ God forgave you" (Eph. 4:32 NIV).

Finding it hard to put others first? Think of the way Christ put you first. "Though he was God, he did not demand and cling to his rights as God" (Phil. 2:6 NLT).

Need more patience? Drink from the patience of God (2 Pet. 3:9). Is generosity an elusive virtue? Then consider how generous God has been with you (Rom. 5:8). Having trouble

HAVING TROUBLE
PUTTING UP WITH
UNGRATEFUL RELATIVES
OR CRANKY NEIGHBORS?
GOD PUTS UP WITH
YOU WHEN YOU ACT
THE SAME.

putting up with ungrateful relatives or cranky neighbors? God puts up with you when you act the same. "He is kind to the ungrateful and wicked" (Luke 6:35 NIV).

The Process

Can't we love like this?

Not without God's help we can't. Oh, we may succeed for a time. We, like Simon, may open a door. But our relationships need more than a social gesture. Some of our spouses need a foot washing. A few of our friends need a flood of tears. Our children need to be covered in the oil of our love.

But if we haven't received these things ourselves, how can we give them to others? Apart from God, "the heart is deceitful above all things" (Jer. 17:9 NIV). A marriage-saving love is not within us. A friendship-preserving devotion cannot be found in our hearts. We need help from an outside source. A transfusion. Would we love as God loves? Then we start by receiving God's love.

We preachers have been guilty of skipping the first step. "Love each other!" we tell our churches. "Be patient, kind, forgiving," we urge. But instructing people to love without telling them they are loved is like telling them to write a check without our making a deposit in their accounts. No wonder so many relationships are overdrawn. Hearts have insufficient love. The apostle John models the right sequence. He makes a deposit before he tells us to write the check. First, the deposit:

God showed how much he loved us by sending his only Son into the world so that we might have eternal life through him. This is real love.

It is not that we loved God, but that he loved us and sent his Son as a sacrifice to take away our sins. (1 John 4:9–10 NLT)

And then, having made such an outrageous, eye-opening deposit, John calls on you and me to pull out the checkbook: "Dear friends, since God loved us that much, we surely ought to love each other" (v. 11 NLT).

The secret to loving is living loved. This is the forgotten first step in relationships. Remember Paul's prayer? "May your roots go down deep into the soil of God's marvelous love" (Eph. 3:17 NLT). As a tree draws nutrients from the soil, we draw nourishment from the Father. But what if the tree has no contact with the soil?

I was thinking of this yesterday as I disassembled our Christmas tree. That's my traditional New Year's Day chore. Remove the ornaments, carry out the tree, and sweep up all the needles. There are thousands of them! The tree is falling apart. Blame it on bad rooting. For two weeks this tree has been planted in a metal bowl. What comes from a tree holder?

Old Simon had the same problem. Impressive to look at, nicely decorated, but he falls apart when you give him a shove or two.

Sound familiar? Does bumping into certain people leave you brittle, breakable, and fruitless? Do you easily fall apart? If so, your love may be grounded in the wrong soil. It may be rooted in their love (which is fickle) or in your resolve to love (which is frail). John urges us to "rely on the love *God* has for us" (1 John 4:16 NIV, emphasis mine). He alone is the power source.

Many people tell us to love. Only God gives us the power to do so.

We know what God wants us to do. "This is what God commands: . . . that we love each other" (1 John 3:23). But how can we? How can we be kind to the vow breakers? To those who are unkind to us? How can we be patient with people who have the warmth of a vulture and the tenderness of a porcupine? How can we forgive the moneygrubbers and backstabbers we meet, love, and marry? How can we love as God loves? We want to. We long to. But how can we?

By living loved. By following the 7:47 Principle: Receive first, love second.

Please listen to heaven's answer. God loves you. Personally. Powerfully. Passionately. Others have promised and failed. But God has promised and succeeded. He loves you with an unfailing love. And his love—if you will let it—can fill you and leave you with a love worth giving.

THE SECRET TO LOVING

IS LIVING LOVED.

THIS IS THE FORGOTTEN

FIRST STEP IN

RELATIONSHIPS.

✳

A Love Worth
Giving to You

But God demonstrates his
own love for us in this:
While we were still sinners,
Christ died for us.
(Romans 5:8 niv)

The Gesture

What's the most wonderfully extravagant gesture someone has ever made for you? Picking you up at the airport in the middle of the night? Sitting by your side in the hospital waiting room? Taking care of your three young children when you so desperately needed a break? Maybe this wouldn't fall into the category of "giving beyond the expected," but at the time and in my situation, the gesture was incredibly precious.

A friend organized a Christmas cookie swap for our church office staff. The plan was simple. Price of admission was a tray of cookies. Your tray entitled you to pick cookies from the other trays. You could leave with as many cookies as you brought.

Sounds simple, if you know how to cook. But what if you can't? What if you can't tell a pan from a pot? What if, like me, you are culinarily challenged? What if you're as comfortable in an apron as a bodybuilder in a tutu? If such is the case, you've got a problem.

Such was the case, and I had a problem. I had no cookies to bring; hence, I would have no place at the party. I would be left out, turned away, shunned, eschewed, and dismissed. (Are you feeling sorry for me yet?)

This was my plight.

I can tell you what I did. I confessed my need. Remember my cookie dilemma? This is the e-mail I sent to the whole staff: "I can't cook, so I can't be at the party."

Did any of the assistants have mercy on me? No.

Did any of the staff have mercy on me? No.

Did any of the Supreme Court justices have mercy on me? No.

But a saintly sister in the church did have mercy on me. How she heard of my problem, I do not know. Perhaps my name found its way onto an emergency prayer list. But I do know this. Only moments before the celebration, I was given a gift, a plate of cookies, twelve circles of kindness.

And by virtue of that gift, I was privileged a place at the party.

Did I go? You bet your cookies I did. Like a prince carrying a crown on a pillow, I carried my gift into the room, set it on the table, and stood tall. And because some good soul heard my plea, I was given a place at the table.

God's Gift to You

And because God hears your plea, you'll be given the same. Only, he did more—oh, so much more—than bake cookies for you.

It was, at once, history's most beautiful and most horrible moment. Jesus stood in the tribunal of heaven. Sweeping a hand over all creation, he pleaded, "Punish me for their mistakes. See the murderer? Give me his penalty. The adulteress? I'll take her shame. The bigot, the liar, the thief? Do to me what you would do to them. Treat me as you would a sinner."

And God did. "For Christ died for sins once for all, the righteous for the unrighteous, to bring you to God" (1 Pet. 3:18 NIV).

Why did Jesus do that? There is only one answer. And that answer has one word: *love*. And the love of Christ "bears all things, believes all things, hopes all things, endures all things" (1 Cor. 13:7 NKJV).

Think about that for a moment. Drink from that for a moment. Drink deeply. Don't just sip or nip. It's time to gulp. It's time to let his love cover all things in your life. All secrets. All hurts. All hours of evil, minutes of worry.

The mornings you awoke in the bed of a stranger? His love will cover that. The years you peddled prejudice and pride? His love will cover that. Every promise broken, drug taken, penny stolen. Every cross word, cussword, and harsh word. His love covers all things.

Let it. Discover along with the psalmist: "He . . . loads me with love and mercy" (Ps. 103:4). Picture a giant dump truck full of love. There you are behind it. God lifts the bed until the love starts to slide. Slowly at first, then down, down, down until you are hidden, buried, covered in his love.

"Hey, where are you?" someone asks.

"In here, covered in love."

Let his love cover all things.

Do it for his sake. To the glory of his name.

Do it for your sake. For the peace of your heart.

And do it for their sake. For the people in your life. Let his love fall on you so yours can fall on them.

OTHERS MAY ABANDON

YOU, DIVORCE YOU,

AND IGNORE YOU,

BUT GOD WILL

LOVE YOU. ALWAYS.

NO MATTER WHAT.

✳

A FINAL WORD

✳

My prayer for you this season of giving is that you will receive God's love and accept your place as a dearly loved child in his heavenly family. Accept the love that came in the form of a newborn babe. Accept the forgiveness and grace bought for you through the cruel, nail-piercing reality of the Cross. Accept his love won for you through the victory of his resurrection. Let this love worth giving fill you, flood you, and change you forever. Live in the knowledge and acceptance of this love. Live loved.

Remember, God loves you simply because he has chosen to do so.

He loves you when you don't feel lovely.

He loves you when no one else loves you. Others may abandon you, divorce you, and ignore you, but God will love you. Always. No matter what.

It is love worth giving. To you.

REFERENCES

"The Season of Giving," is taken from *A Love Worth Giving* (Nashville, Tenn.: W Publishing Group, 2002), "God's No-Pecking Zone," 45, 46.

"A Love Worth Giving," is taken from *A Love Worth Giving* (Nashville, Tenn.: W Publishing Group, 2002), "The 7:47 Principle," 3–9.

"A Love Worth Giving to You," is taken from *A Love Worth Giving* (Nashville, Tenn.: W Publishing Group, 2002), "He Could Have Given Up," 156; and *Traveling Light* (Nashville, Tenn.: W Publishing Group, 2001), 63, 66–67.

"A Final Word," is taken from *A Love Worth Giving* (Nashville, Tenn.: W Publishing Group, 2002), "Unfailing Love," 162.

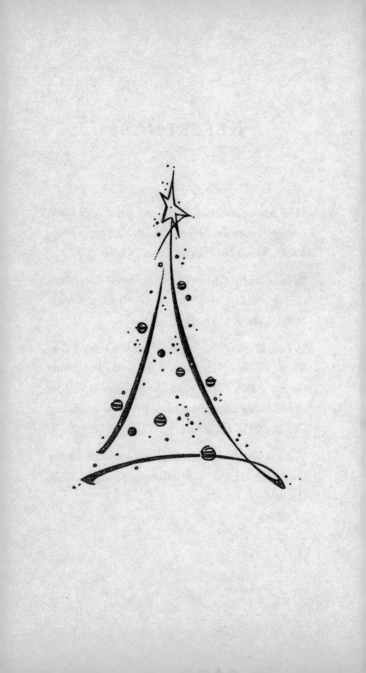